salmonpoetry

Allow the Stars to Catch Me When I Rise

ADAM HUGHES

Published in 2017 by
Salmon Poetry
Cliffs of Moher, County Clare, Ireland
Website: www.salmonpoetry.com
Email: info@salmonpoetry.com

ISBN 978-1-910669-65-5

Cover Image: © *Elenarolau* | *Dreamstime.com*

Cover Design & Book Typesetting: *Siobhán Hutson*

Printed in Ireland by Sprint Print

for Kristen:

My wife, my source, my passion, my love, my clearing to which all paths have led.

Acknowledgments

"1990" previously appeared in *miPOesias.*

Portions of "Archipelago" first appeared in *Arsenic Lobster* and the *Ohio Vintage Matchbook Company.*

"Bill Murray Prepares to Portray D.B. Cooper", "Christopher Walken Prepares to Portray D.B. Cooper", and "Robert Redford Prepares to Portray D.B. Cooper" previously appeared in *FreezeRay.*

"Christmas Eve, 2014" previously appeared in *Mount Island.*

"Corazon", "Into Something Rich and Strange", "On Plans to Build My Daughter a Tipi" and "With Apologies" previously appeared in *The Good Men Project.*

"Driving Through the Blue Ridge, Talking to Myself" previously appeared in *Bodega Magazine.*

"Driving Through the Dark Streets of Lancaster, I Miss My Daughter", "Waking Up Early Sunday Morning", and "On Words Spoken by an Old Man in the Walmart Bathroom" previously appeared in the *Ohio Vintage Matchbook Company*.

"The Geography of Marriage", "Hideous the Scars of Beauty, and I, Impaled", and "On a Piano Discarded by a Pioneer on the Oregon Trail" previously appeared in *The Foliate Oak.*

"Grace" and "The Last Days of Discarded Heroes" previously appeared in *Straight Forward Poetry.*

"Gypsies and Foxes" and "Mystic" previously appeared in *Red Fez.*

"On the Night Ohio State Wins the National Championship, I Return to a Dark and Quiet House" previously appeared in *Midwestern Gothic.*

"A Poem I Dreamed My Wife Wrote About Me" previously appeared in *NEAT Magazine.*

"A Prayer for My Daughter" previously appeared in the *San Pedro River Review.*

"The Town Where Dying is Forbidden" and "The Veneration of Sad Saint Lutra" previously appeared in *Stirring.*

Contents

"I thank You Lord for creating the world beautiful and various and if this is Your seduction I am seduced for good and past all forgiveness"

—Zbigniew Herbert

The Longing for the Dance Stirs in the Buried Life

Sign a covenant of wonder with the world
in the bark of a sycamore;
where there is a charted coast
tack away from it
no matter the dragons drawn
in the blank spaces of the chart;
when you recognize the song
make up new words
even if it means making up a new language
to sing them in;
and when your eyes grow dim
from the smoke from a thousand fires
add more branches and cry
unexplored rivers;

we the empty, the vagabonds, the islands
we the leafrafts, the offkey,
we the forgotten saints
who no one prays to but still stand
in the company of God, our beards
resonant with altarsmoke—

rise.

Lectio Divina

winter in Ohio and all
the riverside saints in their skin-thin robes
beneath a scaffold of stars,
ready to ascend on stairs of sycamore and scrub pine—
on cloudy nights I get lost in my own yard

beneath the ice, beneath the stream,
buried under the riverbed,
the bones of mystics and sunken
fish, like the tombs of pagan kings
guilded with pebbles
as smooth as memory

call me and I'll answer,
tell me what to hear from among
the babel of the birdflocks,
the branches of the ash are full
like time and the sky
at sunset

tonight the horses are kneeling
in the snow, rolling litanies
to their saints beneath
a sky as sad as their eyes

Sacerdotal

last night the stars threw down
their spears, littering
the world with their war

this morning all is dipped
in petrichor, driftwood
bobbing on tides, saltines
soggy on the grass

today I partake of this sacrament
of exile, sing hallelujah
in the key of sparrow

tonight I'm writing notes for
my biographers in fireplace ash
and window mist

tomorrow the horses
will smell the air, with its hints
of tamarack, and their eyes
will roll toward the woods

every moment laden with its
thousand breaths
passes beneath heaven
cold and broken

dawning parousia

Simplicity

When I love, I want to love simply; like unadorned
adobe, plain and smooth and beige, yet warm

beneath the sun and crafted with hands
veined with blue rivers etching endless

cartographical possibilities.
When my bakedbrick love is ready, I will build

a boring house and the sun will make it glow
like the inside of a kiln until sunset paints

over the beige.

Hideous the Scars of Beauty and I, Impaled

for my daughter

the horses' eyes are sad, but not
sorrowful—they look not with fear,
but with the experience of the long married—
they're waiting patiently for the stars to fall
so they might eat them off the tips of the grass

do not cry about things beyond your fingertips—
the deaths of a thousand glinting wasps—
the frosted, the wilted, the broken, the rheumy-eyed—
the world is not dying—it is shedding its skin

do not fear the undergrowth beyond
the first row of trees—it's dark but many have walked
there before you—their footsteps still crunch
if you stop your breathing long enough to listen—
you're never far from something beautiful

when it rains for days, and it appears God forgot
to separate the waters that week, remember me
wherever I am and know that I tried—
the rain doesn't win or lose—it just drops
when it's told to drop, like baby robins from the nest,
some flying, some falling, all changed

The Mountains are High and the Emperor is Far Away

Whisper me the secrets of embers.
Let the moon spin its fantasies
another night, another performance
among the crowded skies.

Remind me tonight of the place
where we entered the water;
show me the sycamore leaves
we sailed, giant coracles;

tell me who I used to be
and speak me into what I'll become.

1990

When I was nine I dressed up for Halloween
as General Norman Schwarzkopf. I outranked
all the other kids in their Teenage Mutant Ninja Turtle costumes
their mothers had purchased at the mall. I proudly wore
my four silver star stickers, the medals made of yogurt lids,
the fatigues a few sizes too big. At recess we shot Iraqis

with sticks, our stomachs full of cafeteria pizza
and chocolate milk. I wrote a letter to the general himself,
I found it fifteen years later in my parents' basement,
like a letter to Santa Claus, unsent but so full
of childhood that the paper crackled
like distant stars and smelled of popcorn

made in the old yellow plastic popper we kept
above the stove. That same year I lost my hearing
in my right ear. I wore a big bubble
around it after my first surgery and kept the gas mask
in the top drawer of my dresser—for months
it still smelled of counting backwards

into blackness. That was third grade, when it was easy
to get Joseph Coffman to throw a chair in class
simply by saying "Bo Jackson sucks." Clearly he had
issues. We didn't know that then, we just thought it was fun
to see someone throw a chair. And besides, everyone knew
that Bo Jackson didn't suck. I had several girlfriends,

some for weeks until we forgot. I was twice married
on the playground. I was in a band, with imaginary instruments
and choreography that included the other members
taking turns kicking me from behind while I sang.
They told me once that I was lucky they allowed me to be
their friend. Some things just stick in your memory

like a bee fossilized in amber or your fingers after
breakfast-for-lunch. I was a good General Schwarzkopf.
Everyone thought so. No one saluted or anything,
but I could see it in their eyes.

While Driving Through the Appalachian Mountains to Meet a Women from an Online Dating Website

for Kristen and others like us

These ridges crouch and slope
like sauropods, their tails entwining
and zigzagging to the edge
of the highway. For miles in the distance
all is spine, rise and decent.

•

Returning home, evening hovering
like the mist around these mountains.
Valleys full of swirling, the bowls
of calumets.

•

Tonight the moon is pushing through,
orchiding the sky.

Homage to Charles Wright

Hoarding the little mounds of sorrow laid up in our hearts,
dust falling between the cracks in our fingers, tomorrow knocking
like an oil-parched engine,
we sing the songs that fall
from constellations. We sing the apples that fall
from the first strong wind in late August.

...

remember us in the ghost hour remember us in our need
remember us in our solstice remember us in our excess
remember us in our headdresses of oriole remember us in our hobbling
remember us in the beauty of the lilies remember us in the
    collapse of mortar
remember us with our fawnspots remember us with our mothwing eyes
remember us who seek to forget

...

We are the Rapture's children
wearing robes in waters stirred by an angel. Peace swoops
like a pipistrelle. To the southwest the clouds
build up into minarets. Peace darts away,
chasing a firefly into the tail-lit darkness.

...

Night with its full syringe,
its epaulet of stars, its milk-
dark flatness, settles in among the pines
like a madness. You can hear the leaves
on the apple tree invert, forming coracles to catch
the sparks that fall when the universe explodes.

    Now is when a great poet would quote
    Wang Wei or Li Po. But I am not a great poet.

So I will lie on my back and allow the stars
to catch me when I rise.

...

God says, watch your back,
cover the hooves of your horses with strips
of shroud and habit, reaching for love
is like reaching for the trunk
of a blue spruce.

Love is only a word, Noah-nude,
stripped of everything sacred, simply
sinew, beard, and joint, sagging
vowels and arthritic consonants.
                    Your accent gave you away,
warming your hands on Golgotha.

...

Pray as though you were praying with someone else's soul
because you are. My child's life is only as sacred
as the life of this baby I hold in one arm, the other
arm pouring the waters of baptism. As drops drip down
her shoulders, her head glistens like an Appalachian bald
drenched in dew. All of our dreams
                    were someone else's first;
all of our originals are imitations; all of our nights,
the ones where we stare at the dark suns on the ceiling,
have been slept through by minds both bolder
and more timid than our own.

If the moon doesn't mind, who am I to say otherwise.

...

A minute of splendor is a minute of ash
and a moment when sunset spreads its scorpion tails
across the grass is a moment to walk among the stings.

A minute of love is a minute of calamus and a moment of silence
is a moment of singing. A minute of pink in the west
is a minute dyed with woad to the east and a moment of wisdom

is a moment of steam rising from rain upon this altar.

Poem For My Father

His wrinkles are deepening, Welsh mines
with no one to work them. His hands stained from cardboard,

topography of delivery routes from fingertip to wrist,
I've never written a poem about him.

I've tried. But there are things I can't seem to write about:
the twin towers, my stillborn brother, the ecstasy of lovemaking,

him. And yet he is in every poem I write. His words, his voice,
his self-mocking, his insecurity. It's all there.

When I was eight, I was obsessed with Desert Storm.
Every day when he came home from work I greeted him

with a second grader's welcome—*did you bring me anything?*
For months, every night it seemed, he brought me a pack of
    trading cards,

Desert Storm ones, with generals and tanks and jets,
and every night I opened them, discarding

the duplicates, sometimes entire packs that I already had,
before going off to continue my play or eat my dinner.

Somewhere, in some layer of a landfill casserole,
are the wrappers of hundreds of packs of trading cards,

the faded cardboard of duplicates, left like sloughed off snakeskins.
But on my bookshelf, near books that somehow I have written,

is a binder. Every single card in the Desert Storm set,
and somewhere tucked in sleeves of plastic, all my father's

dreams, protected, stored, in all my failures and all my victories,
no duplicates, only brand new

gratitude and a song that echoes like the wind through empty mines.

Corazon

i.

Horizoning, tonight my thoughts stretch
and reach further than these ten-mile-away
hills. To love is to lay inside
a deer carcass.

ii.

If all of our loves were embalming agents
love would be worthless. Our love
is decay and decomposition.

iii.

When smegma clogs a horse's teets,
love is the hand to clean where they can't reach.

iv.

Among the Assiniboin, sky buried lovers
reach out to one another
through a galaxy of dead
branches.

v.

What do prophets know of love?
Come, stand on the streetcorner and shout,
"O Great Love! Our hearts
explode with excess magma! The end is love!"

Navigation

feral stars

once I had you so domesticated
you'd eat from my hand

now I call your names
and you refuse to come

Into Something Rich and Strange

Sometimes you can feel the distance
creeping in, continental drift where you wake up
and Madagascar is gone. You know
it was just here. Yesterday you saw it, bobbing
out on the waves; today,
just another disappearance, another channel
wider than the space between the strand
and the corner of sky-sea.

There are days when the sky
chips, the patina
scratches off, rubbed by a dime,
and the horizon splays out
like a dissected frog. On these days, the deckled
edge of evening, the silence of sinking,
leaves you wondering about
floating islands and why the sky resembles
a dropped plate, faulted by falling.

We will not all sleep, but we will all be
awoken. We will not all change,
but we will all be
transformed. Love
digs graves one atop another
and lovers are buried like layer
cakes. The sea changes, the coral grows
with each new wreck, and somewhere beyond the sinking,
a new island appears to someone watching
from another shore.

On Plans to Build My Daughter a Tipi

It will have to be big. Big enough for all three of us
and two or three
dogs. Big enough for toys and a bed
and for the moon and the sound of the creek.

Its poles will need to be lodgepole pine
or sycamore or whatever they have at the local hardware store.
They should be straight and tall
like the rods that held
the ark of the covenant.

The covering will not be buffalo. It will
need to be some sort of canvas,
but a kind that's not too expensive. It will need
to be beige. There should be stakes
to hold it down when the Ohio wind comes through
and tries to get warm inside. There will be no

buffalo skull. No buffalos will be involved in any way.
Or bison for that matter.

We will find a place for it along the creek, an area
I just learned is called the riparian zone.
Our tipi will be a riparian one. She has
no idea what riparian means or the difference
between buffalo and bison. She has no idea
I'm making her a tipi. Which is good,
because then it won't disappoint her when I don't.

I once built a swing—
which is almost like building a tipi.

One day—of course not now, when the winter
skies are full of cement
and the riparian trees
offer nothing of value—we'll lay amidst the teardrops

of evening,
on a floor of grass and count the stars
through the smokehole. She'll be amazed
that she can count them—maybe fifteen
at most—and she'll probably say

"Daddy, those stars are lucky
because we're letting them see in.
Those other stars, the outside ones,
don't know how warm it is in here."

I'll wonder when her eyes
turned that particular shade of spark.

Then her mom will pick her up
and I'll go back inside the tipi and the grass
will smell like her hair and I'll become
one of those outside stars.

And then I'll remember why
I didn't build the tipi.

Love at the Language Creation Conference

after Amorak Huey

Ex nihilo is better than nothing.
Why bother with cognates, with old
embers? Tabula rasa,
things unencumbered by the past.

Love as idioglossia. Love among
the newest buildings
of an ancient civilization. Love
as a new verb in Klingon.

If another language dies
every fourteen days,
we'd better hurry our creating,
each new tongue an opportunity

to forget an old one. How do you say
"Your hips are sexy" in Esperanto?

Farm Dusk

My love and I walk, shoulder to shoulder
with horses. The one she leads
walks in step, gazing ahead. Mine turns
its nose, seeking freedom, a chance
that I am weak. But I am learning.

Watching the horses eat, I stand behind
my love. We look straight and dream
across the trees. Beneath the rising
fog, God's voice sounds like the back legs
of crickets and the faint muffle of horse
breath. I've never heard this accented
God-talk. But I am learning.

Back in their pasture, the horses
linger. They are free; they can graze
or drink or rumble together with hoofbeats
that spread the dew across patches
of clay the color of pumpkin pie. They choose
to groom my love's arm and one nuzzles
my shoulder. Beneath an oat-sprinkled
sky that's missing half
a moon, we are full and new
all at once. I've never understood
horses or how this is supposed to work,
but I am learning.

The sky turns to shades of horse-eye.
The stars walk shoulder to shoulder.
The thousands of nights like this
we searched for answers line up
and trail away to pasture. Tonight, smelling
of old horses and new questions,
we are learning.

Bill Murray Prepares to Portray D.B. Cooper

I think it's all about the bow curve
of the lip. Trajectory
has to be just right, all consideration
given to the weather. If it's cold

I refuse to shoot. When is a parachute
a cross? I should have listened
to my voicemail more closely.

All of the sagaciousness of marked dollar bills,
epistemology. He was Catholic.
Had to be. Look at his eyes.

If the sun sets just right, when I close
my mouth I can see the halo
through the hemlock. I think this
was his motive—this very view.

The wind through the cabin of a plane
is the same as the wind through a parachute
and the way the rain falls through branches
made heavy with the tears of shrouded stars.
I'm getting melancholy in my old age,

like autumn. I know his identity—
but to reveal it would ruin the picture—
I saw him this morning
and last night in the bottom
of an empty reservoir, and I see him
every time the plane door opens.

This masquerade of sleeping pills and army surplus
jackets, the way the moon looks when you've broken
your back, the call of a puma when you know
there are no salmon around this time of year,

asylum of a crowded landing zone. To the fugitive
there's always another sunrise, another jump,
another note to pass another flight attendant.

On Words Spoken by an Old Man in the Walmart Bathroom

"That's the thing with being old. You're liable to wake up one morning dead and not even realize you're dead."

He was at the mirror, wiping his chin, informing me
he had cut himself shaving. He shook his head, smiling
as he said it. I laughed at his words,

until later. Maybe we do wake up one morning
not realizing that we're dead. Maybe the next world
is simply another bedroom, the same smells

of dust and the same shafts of light poking through
curtains and the same empty pillow beside your head.
Maybe we go through whole days before

we notice the change - that the sun is a bit brighter,
the dust clings to our nosehairs with a greater degree
of pungence, the empty pillow sits there decidedly emptier.

Perhaps the old man was on to something, that moment
we cross over may begin with an opening
of our eyes, a stretch, and our feet touching the floor

no longer cold. Such is the way of being old,
I suppose. Where every eye-opening is suspect,
every salmon-bellied sunrise a mirage,

every day a thing to be discovered, proved,
authenticated. To the old man in the Walmart bathroom—
you're alive. The dead have better places to be.

And as You Lay There in Your Blood, I Said to You, 'Live!'

Ezekiel 16:6

In my ears I hear the crashing of every
seventh wave. The fishermen left this morning,
dropplets clinging to their beards, tiny marmosets
in a canopy of vines. Tonight many chairs will be lighter,
many rooms brighter with the absence of shadow.

The talismans of shipbuilders, an amulet
of moon, the charms of the fallen,
glow on these nights when stars are all that return.

If there is no forgiveness of sins without
the shedding of blood, then this sleeping town
remains unatoned. The inky tidal pools, thick

with roe and foam, carry traces of spar
and plankton of hemp and cotton and tea.
Tonight the souls of the naked rise and fall like the fog.

Loading Trucks

Right now Melbourne City is in the 41st minute
against Central Coast Mariners—
a game I care nothing about except
it tells me that somewhere it's warm and sunny
and people are playing soccer

instead of loading trucks in Ohio in the middle
of a December night where Jupiter tops the moon
like a ball approaching the head of a striker.

Tonight all is a flurry of goals.

The Miracle of the U.S. Interstate Highway System and the Precision of Mile Markers

Because *memory believes before knowing remembers.*
Because all of life is charted by ancient navigators,

we've forgotten their glossary of stars, the horizon shimmers
like igneous rocks long cooled, and the maps

are written in a cuneiform no one can read. Creation
is a fixed point. For centuries we've walked

off the mileage, like golfers deciding
between a nine iron and a pitching wedge.

Tell me secret stories of whales with stubby legs,
of feathered lizards and archaeopteryx

learning to fly. There is no temple more sacred
than the Artifice of Precision. No religion

more misleading. Your exit is fourteen miles
away and yet you have no idea where you're going.

The sun sets and the stars dance
around the bonfire the earth is setting.

Tomorrow becomes today somewhere in the darkness
and the steel is cool beneath the dreaming,

sparkling beneath the winks of a million
eyes. The angles are all off, mountains

with gaping holes the size of civilizations,
whole towns the world has forgotten,

and still the salmon spawn and the cedars grow
new bark, and the everything of nothingness

envelops us like a magician's cloak.
Because we're always telling ourselves old stories,

morals so memorized they're almost true.
Tonight the cold is a mural we're all painting.

Something Resembling a Ghazal for New Love

How do I know I'm falling for you? I keep thinking about
    what we would do
if civilization collapsed. I've never hunted.

Last night was the first time I've talked to someone for seven hours
without my attorney present. The lightbulb swung of its own volition.

The moon pokes tonight, reaching its crooked arm around a
    dark circle
that must be earth. I've never figured out how I can see earth
    when I'm on it.

Today I swear I saw a raspberry shiver. It was capped with beachsand
and glimmered like snow on a battlefield. It moved and I saw
    its hairs stand up.

Tonight, in the rubble, I heard you call my name. "Adam,
the stars look like raspberries covered in frost."

The Sea, *or*, A Pair of Shoes in the Middle of the Road

Today's tide looks beautiful, all sunrise
and gusts of wind along the open fields

on either side of the road. There was a sea
here once. A long time ago. Before the sandstone's

memory, its constellations of quartz,
before the bones of whales were pressed

into nothingness and buried inside these hills.
On days like today—short days, unreasonably

warm winter days, days where everything is blown
from west to east and if you're not careful

you'll find yourself carried right into the next
sunrise—you get home and carry in your hair

lingerings of salt, the faintest scent
of a washed-up fish with its open eyes and open ribs,

the places where the land still wells
with the tears of one who has moved on, forgotten,

but still longs to remember the timbre, the moment,
the shoals of everything that was

and the expectation of eschaton.
Today's sunrise looks anciently beautiful like the carved

and open jawline
of a mummified princess. In the middle

of the road, a pair of black sneakers,
and nothing will ever be the same.

Parable

an old man, rotting
from the inside

the stink of his
death, a preamble

        his three sons gather
        to divide
        his wealth

the old man croaks

through
droughted
lips, *fill this*

room completely
and everything I have
is yours

                —night—

first son—

        straw,
        roofs worth of straw,
        enough straw to fill half a room

second son—

        sand,
        stars and stars of sand,
        enough sand to fill half a room

third son—

        a candle
        a match

                an inheritance

Holding On to the Sun

I prefer my days to be hand-held, suns
the size of change, palms lined with blisters
from clutching the day, seeking to still
the rising and setting. It's a good day
when my hands are red and the sky
is full of trout-spots.

Anamnesis

In the library the other day, I found a genealogy file,
a family history of one particular name. It was an ancestor

of mine, so I thumbed through to see how recent the compiler
had gotten. Sure enough, there I was. Right above

my stillborn brother. Our middle names were reversed.
I thought, how odd that something so simple

could be flipped. When flying without instruments
I've heard the sky looks just like the sea.

Our middle names are only different by one letter.
Later that day I read that a human could swim

through the arteries of a blue whale. This world
is full of wonders. Jacob Davis Hughes was born

and died on the same day. It could be argued
that he was far more successful at life than me.

Every morning I lay out the pieces of my life
on this altar and watch for fire to descend.

Tonight the moon spoke to me
in the voice of my dead brother. The voice

I never heard, but immediately identified.
Like swimming through tunnels of cetacean

plasma, some things are understood at a deeper level—
beautiful, meaningless, and truer than blood.

Known and Unknown

I don't know the distance between here and there. I don't know the mileage, or the time, or the number of rivers to be crossed. I don't know the odds of the impossible happening. I can't pretend to know the future, the unwritten words on the wall, the ones in God's handwriting. I only know simple things: the number of hours in a day, the number of days since I've seen you, the geographical location of the aching in my chest. Even with time passing like comet tails, I still know your face, the valleys of your skin, your voice, and your lips that taste of sunset. I don't know if I'll ever see Ireland, or catch a major league foul ball, or love a woman when her hair falls out, but I know that to finally hold you would be the only answer I've ever needed to the only question I've ever asked.

Aubade

This morning I stood on the deck
and stared at the scythe of moon
and the stars that appeared brighter
than they had last night. The sky
held its breath.

I went inside to do the innumerable tasks
of staying alive and returned
to find the east breaking
like a robin's egg. I missed the fading stars
but the moon was still there.

I walked to my car searching
for this last line,
but I never found it.

Driving Through the Blue Ridge, Talking to Myself

Stars surround this mountain, a necklace

of teeth, tomorrow promises rattling
of spears. If I close my eyes, the stars the stars

the stars are empty, like the galeprayers of mariners.
Tonight the moon crests these ridges masquerading

as clouds, peaks through these clouds masquerading
as sauropod backs. Light leaks through the colander

of heaven, and the darkness hides distinction. If tonight
were to whisper to us, would it sound like rumblestrips

on the side of highway 64? Like grainy spurts heard
on radio stations programmed hundreds of miles away?

We all seek harbor. The anchorage the anchorage
the anchorage is full of seabirds. The sky is full

of shading, shoals of clouds/ridges, migratory,
darkness where hours before the sky was the belly

of a coho. One night like tonight I'll be dead. The Milky Way
will have one more pilgrim on hajj. I'm more aware

that one morning the eyes of all my loved ones
will fill with the emptiness of a tide-tossed trout

and these same stars will cross these same ridges
and this same mountain dressed as a witch doctor.

Tonight I am full with an emptiness
only the setting of stars can fill.

Senator Eagleton Upon Reaching Paradise

This isn't my first time conduiting—
energy coursing through me

like an electic eel—there are many faces
on my skull—many angles—

I'm surprised to see
these rooms full of newspapermen—

the streets here remind me of
Jefferson City—I can't find Nixon—

God and I have decided mutually that I
should step aside

for the good of the party—I'm hoping
heaven can win more than Massachusetts—

a cloud just passed
through me—I am finally understood

Song of Solomon

She
I tried to seal up everything you told me
but the leaves were falling
and I got distracted by
their desperation

He
love's thighs swing
like a cluster of grapes,
and I've always been attracted
to things that traverse

She
I want to live on a barren
island where people speak
only in whistles, tones rising and falling
like condors across ravines

He
turkeys will spend hours staring
at the sky, only to drown
in the rain—there's a lesson there
somewhere, probably something environmental

She
I'll stand in the fields today
in the company of foxes catching
fire beneath the harvest sun
singing their hearthsongs

He
from the gates we hang our
second fruits with wire of foxhair
and the plumes of yellow warblers—
our first fruits stopped working long ago

The Watchman

Ezekiel 3

Another bombing mission. Another current
events poem. Another faceless neighborhood

where dogs and children roam through rubble
like the survivors of Jericho. When

will the stars fall like bombs? When will You
get tired of our wars? When will birds sing

from atop our mausoleums and spiders
peek from the cracks in our monuments?

When your thunder shakes our ears, will
we hear words, or just the jostling

of clouds? The people have heard enough
thunder. How long will your message

be either noise or silence? Teach us
a new language or we will die with the wrong words on our lips.

Prayer for My Daughter

I hope one day she understands
that I always wanted
to be there. The currents kept running
the wrong way, these oars
kept splitting, the sun
was always in my eyes,
the stars were full
of typos. But I'm still coming
into port. I hope that's her
standing on the pier, hands
in her pockets, scuffs on her shoes, a seashell
growing out of her ear.

A Cartography of Indigo

past the last bone of the last of an old species, past
the water gaps of nomads, past the lake that glows salmon
in the sunset,
past the sound of the dogpacks, through vapors exhaled
by the sleeping earth, through the places the map has forgotten,
through deserts that dream in petrichor, behind
the vestigial legs of a baleen whale, between the purple
and the blue, between the deep and the not-as-deep,

between the mountain people and the forest people
and the people who sleep on pine needles and the people who hold
memories of their own extinction, beneath barn swallow stars,
beneath the sad wings of angels, beneath votives lit by giants,
beneath the calabash, along the corpse road
with its teeth of monoliths, beyond the furthest shadow
of the ziggurat, beyond a child's dreams but before
their nightmares, beyond abstraction and everything

intangible, above the realm of moles and little people,
above everything that is below

traveler, it is there, in a place you can only reach by holding
your breath beneath the river

On a Piano Discarded by a Pioneer on the Oregon Trail

I read somewhere about families unburdening
their wagons early on in the journey -
pots and pans and furniture lining the ruts
somewhere before the banks of the Platte.

I picture a lone traveler - I don't know why
he's alone, but I choose to think it's because he wants
to be. But he doesn't. I think there's probably a lover
back in Cincinnati. Maybe a creditor in Springfield.
But either way, he's alone.

I think he approaches the piano, upright and scratched,
the only specimen of its kind for hundreds of miles,
the way a horse approaches a newly fallen tree -
hesitant, as if at any moment it could come to life
or throw forth some spark of life that it conceals within
its belly of wood, ivory, and the resonance of memory.

He reaches out slowly, curiously, maybe his chest
rumbles with something resembling laughter.
It's not real laughter of course,
because the only people who laugh alone are insane.
That what he thinks, anyway. No judgement on my part.

The keys make a sound like the keys of a piano
are supposed to make. This surprises him, but he's not sure
why. Perhaps he expected them to be broken
like all things that go on voyages and die
before finishing them. He reaches to play another

but stops. He walks away, humming
that one pitch. I picture him as long as I can until
he disappears on the horizon and the piano
fills with grass, its belly full with one more note.

Meditation

at night all of the stars forget all of the answers
to all of the questions you ask in your sleep

the horses, their God eyes, their ancient,
their flies laying eggs in their teardrops

listen as the pondripples speak
an idioglossia with the bulge-eye frogs

all the world is sown up in crinoline,
threaded with needles stolen from the backtines of bluegill

the arms of the sycamore bear totem tattoos
in patches of algae green and curdled milk

this world, a template of wonders, full
of what is openly hidden and lacking in all subtlety

the children who wake in the night cannot explain
what the fireflies told them before they opened their eyes

the heron's nest along the creek
is stuffed with last year's failures

when everyone's smiles are the wing-eyes of moths,
the future demands our defiance

tonight the smoke from our sacrifices
burns the eyes of angels and tears fall

the geography of your tongue is always changing
and your skin is so new that it shines like cellophane

is it not a miracle that as we sit together, touching along our thighs,
millions of cells within us are dividing unattended

all of the ash are dead along the field edge but they refuse to fall;
stand beside me and we'll whisper resurrection

While Fishing and Catching Only Bluegill I Wonder at the Other Fish in the Pond

after Kathryn Nuernberger

I once pulled in a bluegill roughly twice the size
of my hook. It had bitten down and the barb had gone in
its throat and out its eye. This bothered me.

Our pond is only bluegill. They've eaten all the eggs
of catfish and bass. I hear the young bluegill at night
laughing about this. They are not bothered.

I've heard it said that once God let the bluegill
name names and write the songs, that their silence
is a matter of things stolen. This bothers God

and the chieftains of the bluegill. Their warlords
in the algae, at the base of the water lilies,
respond with genocide. This would bother the sunfish

but they are only a memory. After a couple minutes
of tugging, I've freed my captive and its eye
remains whole, unbroken. Unbothered,

it takes flight from my hand, its spines splayed
like a sail, flopping like an uncoordinated gymnast
back into the water where it hangs suspended

beneath the algae for a moment, then snaps
to life and swims off into the murkiness
of the pond, whose waters become night

after six inches of depth. Creation does not bother
with the past. Among the warrior bluegill
there are no historians.

Grace

Angel with the sword, hold off
another moment. I just made
love to my wife and we'd like to lie here,
a grapevine and an ash,
a twist of fiber, sinew,
and curvature. Please hold off longer,
for earlier we stood beneath
the cloud-blurred stars—pockets
of spark amidst the smoke-sky—and watched
the horses doing nothing in the fields,
heads low, facing north, doing nothing more
beautifully than anything has ever
done nothing before. Hold off with
your cutting down and your famining,
tomorrow night is supposed to be clear
and all I want from life is to sleep
in a world where love is made
and horses stand, sleeping beneath
the bleached arms of a sycamore.

Regret

If I'd known that was the last piece of candy in the bag
I'd have enjoyed it more. I wouldn't have rushed it
down my throat and into the agitator of my stomach,

where it's already a memory to my tongue, a few particles
lining my esophagus. I'd have relished it, tasted it
beyond the usual time it takes to chew and swallow.

I'd have learned its flavor, utilizing the full range
of my taste buds—dull they may be. But the moment
has gone to my intestines, where there is little room
for sentimentality.

On the Unreliability of Clouds

Your eyes aren't fluttering--angels are dancing
on them. Your lids, lined with topographical maps

of river deltas, hide the darkness, hold
in the light. Did I tell you about this morning?

The clouds looked just like a distant mountain range.
They looked so permanent, so stable. I looked

away and they shifted, broke, my faith too weak
to keep them from moving. Tonight

I keep staring, fearing that if I look away
you'll shatter, dissemble into chimney breath.

So I watch, quiet as an old battlefield
that still speaks to itself in a whisper. "For love is

strong as death, the very flame of the Lord."
Tonight the angels shuffle a holy litany

as I hum a song to still the clouds.

Mystic

Tonight I shined my headlights
on God. He was standing in the road,
thin as smoke. I know it was him,
I'd know those hollow eyes anywhere.

When he jumped
off the bridge, I thought the trees
would catch him, but I found him later,
crawling along the guardrail,
a gash on his head, an old elbow-patch coat,
and one sock, mumbling something
in a language I remembered
forgetting. Now I'm in bed

and God is somewhere in the city
beneath the river, lighting
candles among last year's fallen
leaves and placing coins in the mouths of fish.

I stare at the ceiling and God
looks down on me with the sad eyes
of a rich man and the smile of a beggar.
And the light from a million bonfires
burns holes in my blankets
until my eyes water, overflowing,
and God casts his nets

one eye to the other,
catch and release,
catch and release.

Encouragement

A man perched, wingless falcon,
seventeen floors above 92nd.

The crowd waits, stomachs
sucked in, muscles contracted, silent.

A man's voice: *If you're going to jump,*
jump. I'm late for work

and I've already used this excuse once.

Robert Redford Prepares to Portray D.B. Cooper

As I recollect, the ground smelled of leaf mush
and the trees ladled water
down my back. I'd try and run between
the drops, bouncing from clearing to clearing
beneath the barking of squirrels.

I hid among the craters and tried not to look
them in the eye. The clouds blended between
forest and sky and everything seemed
misplaced. Now my face

is a topographical map of the region.
Each new crevice a new ridge, a new valley,
a new hiding place. The first person a fugitive
hides from is himself. I'll make sure

he never finds him. Alone in this cathedral,
this sacred grove of rain,
the difference between living and dying
is the difference between myth and pretending.

I imagine he hasn't seen the moon in forty years.
That changes a man. I imagine he hasn't smelled
a woman in forty years. I imagine he misses
the moon more. But at night I bet he dreams
of features more feminine than the moon's.

To dream his dreams—that's the key.
To see with his eyes, the smoke coming closer,
taking form as clouds through a spruce,

the fingers reaching like a woman half-remembered,
reaching but never touching.
I woke up this morning and couldn't remember
the smell of the moon.

Ember Days

Days like these, when the sky is too far
to hold and the clouds are too close to see,

wrap themselves in the feathers of an egret,
plumed in shades of calamus and ash and dare

unfortunates to hope for death
that does not include breathing water. That's foolish,

of course. All things do not happen
for a reason. There is no reason for most

of what happens in our lives, just smoke
from a thousand fires left untended. Only you

can prevent them. Except you can't. Today the wind offers
seven ways to kill a wolf. One through six involve

attrition. The seventh is written in an ancient dialect
of Chumash. When these hills glow in shades of war

bonnet, when they dance, shirtless, their rattles hissing
rain through empty branches, they'll shrug

shoulders sinewed with grapevines and wearing epaulets
of discarded nests. Listen and you'll hear it,

the crackling of green wood. These days of smoldering,
days of spent coals, days of lingering heat,

these days where we wait for a voice to confirm everything
we've been thinking. We hear our echo and call it God.

If this day dissolves, like a pill in warm water,
is there anyone who will drink it?

No, not one. Come, Lord Jesus. Amen.

After Listening to a Country Song and Missing My Love, I Think of the Future

One night soon we'll lie on the grass, horse-nipped
blades brushing our backs. We'll stare into the compound eyes
of heaven, touching at shoulder, hip, knee, ankle.

If we hear music, we'll dance. If we taste sweetness,
we'll drink. If we see life projected across the obsidian east,
we'll live it. If we feel the creekstone smoothness of our skin,

we'll grab it, holding the pommel of a future both fierce
and beautiful and we'll not let go. That night you and I will swim
through starshoals, wade among the wishes, safe beneath

the hand that lit those flickering torches, that scrawls its signature
in constellations. We'll fall asleep to the weeping
of the willow in the pasture. Covered in dew, singing dreamsongs—

This love, this abstraction, this defier of definitions,
this longing, this hunger, this dream-giving,
this light-bringing, this future-unwrapping,
this newness, this temple, this living.

The Creator still creates, the Fisherman still trawls
the Lover of our souls still rocks us to sleep,
as our eyes flicker with somnolescent visions,
we pray the Lord our love to keep.

Safe in our estuary, safe in our anchorage,
safe in our moon-watered bay;
secure in God's unwrestled blessing,
asleep above His leftover clay.

We'll hold each other in the cooling air,
our touch, our breath, our love—a prayer.

Three Hearts

While driving, hand on
the wheel, upside-down
Welsh tattoo around my wrist
Awenydd Milwr Offeiriad

Turning, little muscles jumping,
a ripple of letters, Welsh waves,
the orange lightfield of the DuPont plant
reflecting fire on the Kanawha.

I drive past the thinning hair
of February mountains. All of these
miles, all of these roadprayers,
all of these lines typed into
a cell phone; I rub my eyes, count
down the hours, hear
God in the static between stations
Poet Warrior Priest

•

Tonight I stood in the darkness
of the house, beneath the living room skylight,
beneath the mostly full moon, beneath
the mostly silent heavens, and looked
for something profound, something poetic,
something to give symbols to the darkness,
the mostly full moon, the mostly silent heavens.

Instead I turned on a light to scrawl
these lines in a pen that puts out too much
ink, tipping each letter with an expanding
puddle of witchcraft, in a handwriting that would never
cut it in a monastery, in a notepad
filled with flotsam and the ramblings of a man
reading too much Ezekiel. Bereft of lighted epiphany—
return to dark.

Apparently My Grandparents Grew Up in a Charles Simic Poem

My grandmother was born in a farmhouse in 1938.
She weighed two pounds and while waiting for the doctor
they placed her in a cotton-lined shoebox
and tucked her behind the woodstove, feeding her
with an eye dropper. My grandfather had St. Vitus Dance
in sixth grade, missed the whole school year.
The next year he walked into seventh grade
and they let him stay. He was poor
and kids once kicked him while he drank
from the drinking fountain, breaking his tailbone.

Lives later, my grandmother still sings
in the church choir, my grandfather
in the heavenly one. Lives from now,
my grandchildren will tell about how I
once had hair, grew up without internet,
and loved a red-haired woman so much
that I burst into flames myself.

Christmas Eve, 2014

The Scriptures tell us that time can be
filled, like a pinata, ready to burst
at the thumping of certainty, the readiness
of a thousand angels. Pregnant,
creaking and groaning like an old monk's knees,
anticipating newness and sundering,

(this has nothing to do with the rain)

time a heavy cloud. Perhaps none of this is accurate
and instead all of our days are shaped
like a cosmic serpent, spread out for space-miles
or coiled like galaxies that collapse
at their edges, stardust

hanging like so many shining
curtains in the windows of forever. There are those
who say that time is without shape,
but we know this to be
wrong. For time is something to be grasped,
tiny newborn fingers

around a father's beard. Today
is a bow, tomorrow an arrow, all of our yesterdays
the pulling of a string.

Driving Through the Dark Streets of Lancaster, I Miss My Daughter

She is three and on vacation with her mother.
The moon is covered with wax paper.

Just off the road the fallen tree limbs await
collection, the grass beneath them already brown.

She sleeps in a cabin in Tennessee. Half
of our town still sleeps without street lights.

The storm was dry and silent
save for bark snapping, signal flags in the wind.

She'll return next weekend.
We'll uncover the moon. It will smell of cooling bread.

The Geography of Marriage

My new wife and I are separated
by four hundred miles, several rivers,
and uncountable ridges, rises, hills,
mountains, all slowly declining
in their broccoli-topped beauty.
For three months and eleven days our marriage
has been one of driving through
the fog-filled valley of the Ohio and the lumbering
Blue Ridge. I flipped my car one night,

asleep at the wheel outside Ronceverte.
Separation nearly killed me. Four more months
and my growing familiarity with central
West Virginia radio stations will come to an end.

Distance is best measured in mountain
peaks and bridges. I'll see her again in forty-three
barges and a few more inches of moon.

The Veneration of Sad Saint Lutra

i.

Sad Saint Lutra—
patron of riverside sycamores with their ivory arms,
of incomplete constellations, their borders broken by oak
and maple,
of streamstones stacked on sandbars between the banks,
of fallen trees stretching across the water, their roots the
homes of crawdads,
of clearings in the forest where we pitch our tents in sight
of our porchlight,
of the silent, the still, the sleeping, the star-staring

ii.

when water drops from leaves
and stars, they are the tears of Sad Saint Lutra;
the thousand holes along the banks,
the places touched by the staff of the holy one;
the current in the middle of the stream,
the wake of his water walking;
the pink in the sunset, coals for his cooking-fire

iii.

when the hawk builds its nest in the top of the sycamore,
it's Sad Saint Lutra who supports the limbs
and holds up the chicks when they take their first plunge;
it's the good saint who sings
your children to sleep when they hear the coyotes
and know what their howls mean; he sits at the feet
of the ancients when the fire fades to embers

iv.

some days he goes missing, lost among the reeds
where the bank is a root-covered wall above
the bend; no one knows where he goes

but a fire of pine and old hay will bring him back
every time—the sparks spraying
and popping reminds him of stars
at the beginning of time—he's heard their secrets

v.

if you touch his forehead, they say
you'll be able to find the sleeping places
of foxes—silvery ones who know how to hide
among the unlit boulders and beneath
the brushpiles; no one knows if this is true
as his forehead
is guarded by angels

vi.

I heard him once, walking through the long grass
of the bottom field, but I didn't see him,
all I saw was a cloud of fireflies
as thick as truth; tonight the stars
smelled like river mud
in the fur of a dog, the smell
all thick with current and decay

vii.

a thousand feast days, a dozen
resurrections, a million minor
miracles, hundreds of totems,
an amulet hung from the Pleiades;
his litany written in the tongue
forgotten by infants, remembered
by the dying, still spoken beneath the stream.

Margaret Thatcher

Margaret enters Paradise and is greeted
by Bobby Sands. "Would you like to feel
my side? My canyon of ribs?
Feel the fossils of my hands?"

Margaret looks at him, as one trying
to remember, searching his eyes for something
familiar, the muscles around her mouth
twitch in recognition, "What are you doing here?"

Bobby smiles, "Blessed are they
who hunger and thirst."

Becalmed

I can't decide if you're the sail
I raise and fill with breath
or the oars I grip
with spent and quivering hands.

Either way, the stars,
the stars, all the pretty stars,
are wandering and we,
well, we

The Hermit Retires

I climbed
out of my tree stump
with the lean-to roof—
the sun was a silent
movie from the '30s.

Twenty-seven years,
four months and sixteen days
is long enough
to learn to hear
the epics of leaves, their

chants of ancient quests
from the top of maples to the bottom
of the brook with its bed of decay
and roe. I said goodbye
this morning to the ash

of twenty-seven years,
four months and sixteen days,
to the roots around me
that have grown like the calluses
on the inside of my feet—bigger

but completely devoid of feeling.
Today I've burnt
my home, my possessions.

Twenty-seven years,
four months and sixteen days
I haven't heard
my own language
except once when downwind

of a helicopter. In those days
I was fluent in every tongue

of ripple, every dialect
that spread itself
from bank to bank,

pushing coracles of leaf
and water bug. This morning
was my last of listening,
from now on I wake
like everyone else—with words

on my lips and last night's wine
on my breath, and a ringing
in my ears that I'll call conversation.

Headline: Sixty-Nine People Die After Drinking Contaminated Beer at a Funeral in Mozambique

Supposedly the poisoning agent was crocodile bile.
When I see a news story that mentions
crocodile bile, I always read it. Funeral
mourners, drunk on pombe and crocodile bile,
flooding Mozambican emergency rooms,

victims like common chickens
of the digestive juices of a crocodile.
Whether this is true or not, I don't know.

But then again, I don't know much about truth.
Or crocodile bile. What I do know

is the taste of vomit. The way the dead
change color—like a morning dawn
where the clouds block the sun, just darkness
transitioning to greyness. The pull

of a tragedy at the very moment
of the commemoration of a tragedy—
a kind of tragedy matryoshka,

a little more hurt inside of a bigger hurt
burning like bile, breaking down
everything it touches.

A Poem I Dreamed My Wife Wrote About Me

I wonder what you're dreaming
about, your eyes fluttering
like horseflies
from flank to flank, dodging
the tail. My guess is
it has something to do with

sex. You're sleeping
through the rain on the farmhouse
roof, drops pinging
their springsongs, lyrics
tap, dervish, sprawl
like our daughter at her dance class,

askew. Your mouth
moves, you mumble,
your breath escapes like a musk

from under the house,
a trapped skunk. I love you
anyway. You'll wake soon

and want to make love. After
you brush your teeth
I'll give you something
to put in your poems.

Sometimes the Moon is Simply a Rock Held in Place by Earth's Gravity

This pain in my belly is not,
in fact,
a metaphor.

It has nothing to do with custody
battles, or late mortgage payments,
or the fact that I

just ate half a bag of chips
and four cheddar dogs.

Metaphor or not,
I'm not sleeping.

I Am Become Death

I shouldn't be surprised anymore when my body bursts
into a thousand sparrows. These things are commonplace,
like a turtle laying its eggs in glass and beards of coconut.

Whenever I dissemble into escadrille, a squadron
of maple pods, whenever my shadow shifts the sky,
I link feathers with myself and feel the shattering of worlds.

Twelfth Night

January 5, 2013—for my wife

Tonight, with the tree by the curb, waiting,
we join its departure. Shed of ornamentation

we'll stand, naked and alone, anticipating the arrival
of forest. Tomorrow brings an ending. The stars

are a colander, God peeking through, crying tears
of meteor. Tonight we are divided by mountains,

rivers, a million sleepers, stretches of highway
that bear remnants of fragmentation, enough

heartbeats to fill this empty house with blood. You're
thinking that this is dark. But this darkness

shines, reflects off orca-bellied clouds,
illuminates. I have fallen in love

with the reflection of light. Tonight, my fertile
tears, my sighs of fire, speak the language

of adoration. Hundreds of miles, but a journey
ended. Tonight, what you will

be is an imaginary warmth in my bed, a glimmer in the corner
of my eye, a dream from which I wake, trembling,

a lingering of notes.
Play on.

How Many Nights

After Galway Kinnell

How many nights
have I lain in my failure,
eyes wide open, seeing
nothing.

Creator, Maker-of-no-Mistakes,
I'm not calling you deficient,
or a liar—I'm simply
trying to see the ceiling.

Tonight I read Ezekiel
and a book on creating
fictional worlds
while holding

a kitten.
Search for meaning all you want, but holding
a sleeping kitten is escape
enough for me.

What Prayer Is

A sixty degree day in an Ohio February. A cigarette butt
tossed from a moving car, exploding
into bursts of disintegrating meteor or adding to the coast
of Hawaii. A hawk perched on a dead deer, not eating,
just staring the vultures in place. A gallows
moon, star swinging beneath, my daughter
trying, but unable to reach. The failure
of instinct while considering
that first kiss. Bodybuilders with no necks,
turning their entire bodies to respond to a call, like
a mechanized wheelchair. That moment
before sunset where the sky holds up
an atomic dime and the world looks away.

The Last Days of Discarded Heroes

Sometimes the last meal is burdock, sometimes
a seven-day-dead pigeon. Sometimes they're alone,
through intent or because no one can find them
on account of not looking. Their shoulders

are usually parabolas, their tongues hairier than most,
their eyes—lemur big yet barely seeing—dim
from the habit of no longer searching. For some,

their fingers are bent, like a long-time weight lifter's,
during handshakes they pierce the other's palm,
a stigmata. One day fathers will tell stories

to their inattentive children, passed down
from their inattentive parents, of legends, heroes,
ones who held worlds and armies, ones who dreamt

and woke too soon. Let us praise famous
forgotten ones, the ones who have no feast days
because no one noticed their death.

On the Night Ohio State Wins the National Championship, I Come Home to a Dark and Quiet House

Tonight, somewhere on High Street, a couch is burning.
It's probably a plaid couch—every college couch
seems to have the same pattern. Somewhere around it
are students, revelers before this molten fabric
and wood. Their faces glow like Moses'.
They breath in the pyric smells, maybe throwing
on a can of beer just for the hiss and sudden rise of flame.

I kneel in the darkness of the living room
until my knees stiffen and my eyes burn.
Our couch is leather, I have no desire to set it on fire.
But eventually all things must be consumed.

In the inkwell of our house, the silence
of a cenote, the smell of flames in my arm hair,
my socks, the carpet. Tonight we hold up
trophies, things that burn, empty hands.

Christopher Walken Prepares to Portray D.B. Cooper

I've tamed lions, did you know that?
Real lions.

To see a savage beast subdue its own instincts,
its own desire to rip out the throat of the nearest prey,

is to understand how to portray a man
because every man ever born is a killer;

every day every man decides to put down
that instinct that tells him to take the life

of the nearest enemy. Every man. Every day.
You know that?

To jump
from a plane doesn't take courage.

Asking for extra parachutes is the antithesis of courage.
He was no lion tamer.

Lions know what's been taken from them.
Their eyes are King Lear's. Othello's.

This guy, this poor chump, I know
what happened to him. But it's not good

for the script. So we make up lies
and cover the truth with leaves to hide the blood.

At the end we'll all gather around a cedar
and sing "God Bless America."

Two Days Before Our First Anniversary

I could write enough poems to fill
a thousand notebooks, but my best ever written
will be lived in loving you.

I am not a dancer, but if the stars
can move in choreographed rhythms,
if our daughter can learn to skip
without falling down, then one of these days
I'll get the hang of leading.

November looks different this year,
getting to see you every morning
and every night; November, with its
red hair and skin as smooth
as sycamore bark.

If love survives in dank catacombs,
in cells and ruins, if love speaks
unspoken languages, if love sometimes sings
in dissonance, then surely love
is here, on a farm with two dogs,
four cats, and four wet horses, sometimes
a daughter, and two people--one outstanding
in being undeserving and one overflowing with grace.

Silence

Tonight the silence
dangles, a comma,
separating,
joining,
but never finishing.

On National Stepfamily Day I Read Ezekiel 32

"They went down to the realm of the dead with their weapons of war"

A prophecy against Egypt, against Pharaoh,
against arrogance and power. Nations, whole armies,
descending buried beneath their shields like wasps
covered by tea cups. Put aside your sword

and I'll sleep on mine. Tonight the tents of the sleeping army
are inside the walls
of our house. We sleep unsteady,
as if in coracles.

I've gone down once. I've seen the scattered warriors,
the proud warlords humbled by time. Tonight
may our war be fought in our peacemaking,
may the casualties be heavy and our resurrection complete.

I will not go under clutching my weapons,
holding on to the end. I let go so I might hold you tighter.

Micronation

I know a man who keeps a country
in his barn. All of his papers are in order: his constitution
based on that of New Zealand.
He has unrestrained power. An absolute monarchy.

My micronation is a failed state. My borders are not secured
yet not threatened. My population is one, occasionally two,
never more than three. My chief export is the echo
of my voice cascading down a canyon. I import
everything. My beaches are littered with used
needles and the tide smells of insulin. I filibuster
all of my proposals. My papers are in shambles.
The constitution has been suspended for years, I rule
with a fist made of styrofoam, its finger pointing,
its slogan screaming my solitude. Today I celebrate

my despotism. My kitchen table is a block
of Naples on garbage strike. I go to bed and the chorus
of advisors begins. I wake to quiet them.

I fear a revolution is brewing.

A Poem Is a Prayer

after Christian Wiman

Sometimes when the evening enters
the water, the shore wonders
if it will ever return to morning—

two, maybe three times, the rocks
along the coast have woken to darkness
where there should have been light—

these things are unexplainable.
Inked in the darkness of an uncertain
return, the trees and the stones and the waters

still as a dead swan watch
for the salmon to return to the sky.
From the reeds as stiff as Jericho's walls

spring peepers pray unrequited incantations.
All of creation groans
through clamshell teeth

and relief is a metered myth.

Separation

i.

There are whales alive today that were born
before *Moby Dick*. Isn't that strange?

Tonight I saw the moon leaking
its light into pools of milk

and something resembling the color
of tidal foam. I'm fascinated

that somewhere geriatric whales
are swimming through the same

moon-tugged tides, the same shoals
of wonder, the same grinding teeth

of liquid eternity. Tonight this bed
feels like keelplanks, opening

and closing like the ribs of a whale.
I stare at the ceiling and know

that nothing is as it seems.
The moon and ancient whales

sing their harmonies and I choose
to believe that someone somewhere

hears them.

ii.

Tonight my daughter said that the sun
was beneath the grass. She's six
and doesn't know how things work.

Tonight I laid on the couch, trying to sleep, staring
at yesterday and the day before that,
everything buried beneath the grass.

I'm thirty-three and I don't remember what it's like
to know where the sun goes at night.

iii.

Tonight my prayers
are a house built
with the bones of birds.

Tonight the stars roar
their gravity somewhere
beyond our ears.

Tonight the wind
is louder than God
has ever been.

I never see the dew fall
but every new sunrise
my feet are wet.

Gypsies and Foxes

I have too many poems
about stars, about the moon,
about sycamores and horses.
I'm tired of them all.

I need more poems about gypsies.
And foxes.

I hate the sky with its blankness
and possibility. I hate the sycamores
with their arms all askew
like Moses' hair.
I hate the horses and their hunger.

Instead I want to write about
Greenland. About otters.
About gypsies raising foxes
and training them to steal
the bread from bakeries
and the babies from their cribs.

No more skies of smokescreen
stars and moons of parchment paper.
No more sycamores haunting
the creek or horses
snapping grass in the quiet night
beneath a colander of stars.

No, only women who wear red,
bowls of oranges, pangolins,
and miniature gypsies on the backs
of foxes.

The world has too many skies.
The woods have too many tall trees,
scapula white and top-nested.
The pastures have too many horses.

What I wouldn't give for the tail of a fox
and the movements of a gypsy, wandering
like stars from light to light.
Then I could forget about the heavens
and the trees and the horses with their oak brown
eyes of prophets and their reminders

that all things return to those foolish things
we have the arrogance to love.

With Apologies

After making love we are footsteps,

the kind that lead off into snow, the ridges
of our shoes prying up lines of powder

that stick to our boots and are carried
into the house to melt on the tile floor.

Of course, everything turns to water.

We stay still in the inkwell of our room,
touching along the length of our yesterdays,

fingers tracing the tomorrows of our
hip bones. The dawn is six and a half hours away

and two months overdue. You walk so much
faster than me, but your prints are closer

together. Together we are falling
asleep, scuffing our feet in dreams

that remind us of reality and all its varied
fictions. Tonight we burned our books

on the bonfire of forgiveness and we'll wake tomorrow
covered in ash and wind drops.

This house burns. Our footprints remain. We can't always
tell which direction they're going.

But still we walk, our backs enflamed with molting
feathers—

angels or egrets.

Archipelago

driving, full of the emptiness
of sky after a storm,
the remorse of a vacuous horizon
cadmium'd in shades of cutthroat trout,
the apology of stars
blinking their tears, holding out
their fiery fingers,
unseen yet present, offstage
but the curtain is lifting

all of our mythologies are copies;
our sooted wings are secondhand;
we soar crowded skies, hijackers
floating like raindrops, hanging
pinecones among the spruce;
your old men will dream dreams
and your young men will see visions;
tonight we look at the stars
in their archipelagos
and pattern them into belief;
when the eschaton comes, we'll hold
out our hands and catch the falling
drops, like dew from treebound
apples; with tattoos of anchors
and stars, with spirals around our eyes,
we'll dip our hands in the waters,
raise them to our nose and lips
and know the direction of home;
until then, we sail beneath strange
constellations, into and out of
the wind

the kingdom of heaven suffers violence
and the violent take it;
I see you there, a car-hit fox,
fierce with ruined back legs; you snarl,
fear in your rage, streaked with bloodshades;
I hate love and its shattering of bones

with exceeding joy,
both now and forevermore,
dreaming grandfather's bass—
legato, fermata, crescendo—
the rumble of distant thunder,
a reminder that all things linger—
the pressing of a piano pedal
until our memories hum a descant
no one else can hear

tonight the moon is full of ink,
waiting for the month to be written
in increments of cuticle;
proverbs written in the accent of an exile,
azaleas unfolding overnight,
a cenote ready for offerings to fugitive gods,
the only son inquiring of the ram

laying in the demidark, summoning
ancient warsongs in as many
dead languages I can think of;
hearing whispered transmissions,
conversations on frequencies
never meant to be tapped -
domestic squabbles disguised
as sacred incantations

outside, beneath the cloudseas,
wet horses like monks to midnight prayer,
I am seduced beyond forgiveness
as they hunch their matins

the pond ripples, bubbles, splishes
its secrets; in the water only clouds,
a setting spring sun, the earthworm
impaled, offering no answers

arise from the dead, o sleeper
the morning is dark and heavy
with dew, the trees, the trees

their grapeshot, their galaxies;
the root of all sin is self-deception;
every morning I begin the day in sin,
whispering sonnets to the mirror,
regurgitations,
plagiarisms,
hoaxes
more ancient than truth—
in the morning, when the moon undresses
and the woodpecker knocks and the trees
stand heavy along the creek, for an instant—
something

dusk with its soundtrack of horsehymns,
the sundering of tiny
grassroots, the clipchipcrack
of rending, strewn garments amidst the ashes,
all of creation groans,
listen and respond,
an incantation of mumbles

all is kenosis, I used to think
life was about filling what was empty;
now I realize it's about emptying
what was full—*reveal your presence*
and let the vision and beauty
kill me—death by a thousand
surrenders

some nights I go to bed smelling of embers,
my legs sticking together
with sweat, dust, and remnant,
I wake in the morning, cutting myself
into pieces, waiting for your fire
to descend upon this altar;
the hope of resurrection lies in ruins
left when fire dies

there are only so many ways one can talk about sunsets,
but horses have a different language;
tonight my eyes
heard their hymns and my skin
rose like the blades of grass slowly growing
to swallow the sun
and the horses were simply there,
as there as the grass and the fence and the sun
doing its best Icarus, fading into a sea
of hills, just there
with their psalms more real than anything has ever been

look for the back of the sun,
like Moses seeing the train
of God's robe, glory is best observed
with eclipse glasses, I'm worried
about the spots spreading across
the sky like fleas

amulets hanging from totems of ash and rain,
the fullness of time, the ripeness of raindrops,
today is sacred somewhere,
to somebody, somewhere a saint
is venerated, somewhere a child
presents a nursery rhyme as holy writ;
this catacomb life, lived beneath
the raucousness of footfalls,
empty
and yet full
scattered
and yet gathered
alone
and yet surrounded

bonfires speak in tongues
of ancient woodlands, of old fence posts,
whispers of hedge and the ecstatic
shouts of conifers dervishing their sparks;
this chapel of stone and ash,
residue of remembrance,
cold with the memory of heat

the war is known from its dispatches,
reports from the front
are unreliable; Uriah returns
with orders from the king,
a tactical retreat; blood
calls out to blood

some nights the stars smolder, like God
covered their embers with wet leaves,
the great bonfire of heaven
suddenly smokes and you can almost hear
the sparks snapping and the wind carrying
bits of starflame
from one end of the night to the other

driving tonight beneath an enormous
harvest moon, the color
of old newspaper, with each turn in the road
it gets smaller; tonight's yellow, shrinking moon,
so full of pathos—too much, moon,
show, don't tell

Legacy

When I die
remember

my victories, my list
of vanquished enemies,
my admirers and family.

Remember the rocks
flung into deep waters,

the way I always hoped
to accurately describe
the scrub pine.

Shadow people, faces dimly lit,
forget my failures—I fear

they are all
that will outlive me.

Litany

in and out,
        wherever,
always be

when I whistle,
        be
the words
my mouth is
        holding

when it rains,
        be
the drop that falls
from the eave
        down
the back of my shirt

of course I won't
        forget—
even if it's cloudy
for days
        and
the stars move on
without me

ADAM HUGHES is the author of two previous poetry collections, *Petrichor* (NYQ Books, 2010) and *Uttering the Holy* (NYQ Books, 2012), as well as the forthcoming *Deep Cries Out to Deep* (Aldrich Press, 2017). A former pastor, he lives and writes on a farm in the foothills of Virginia's Blue Ridge Mountains with his wife, daughter, five horses, two dogs, and four cats.